HENZE

at the

ROYAL NORTHERN COLLEGE
OF MUSIC

HENZE

at the
ROYAL NORTHERN COLLEGE
OF MUSIC

CONVERSATIONS
Edited by Douglas Jarman

in association with

Published by Arc Publications
Nanholme Mill, Shaw Wood Road
Todmorden, Lancs. OL14 6DA

Design by Tony Ward
Printed at the Arc & Throstle Press
Nanholme Mill, Todmorden, Lancs

ISBN 1 900072 27 0

ACKNOWLEDGEMENTS
The RNCM Henze Festival (Artistic Director,
Professor Edward Gregson) was organised in as-
sociation with the BBC Philharmonic and the
Goethe Institut, Manchester.

The publishers wish to thank:
Hans Werner Henze, the staff and students of the
RNCM and other musicians for allowing them-
selves to be photographed at rehearsals during the
Festival;
Fausto Moroni Henze for the cover photograph
of the composer, taken at the composer's home in
Marino, Italy in Summer 1998.

CONTENTS

EDITOR'S PREFACE
Douglas Jarman

This book is one of three volumes published to celebrate the visit of Hans Werner Henze to the Royal Northern College of Music in November 1998, and is a record of some of the activities that took place during the week that Henze stayed in Manchester as Composer in Residence at the College.

The text of the book consists of three conversations. Two of them are transcriptions of public conversations with the composer. The first, between Henze and the Editor, was recorded on Friday 13 November, immediately before a concert that included the UK premières of *Gypsy Tunes and Sarabandes* and the revised Sixth Symphony. The second conversation, between Henze and Peter Sheppard Skaerved, took place the following evening, Saturday 14 November, before the UK première of the First Piano Concerto and a rare performance of the Eighth Symphony.

The other conversation was between the Editor and Gary Walker and Jennifer Hamilton, respectively the conductor and director of a production by the RNCM of *Pollicino*, Henze's opera for children, which opened the Festival in Manchester. This production involved students from the RNCM, the

RNCM Junior Strings Project and four local schools – Chetham's School, Manchester High School for Girls, Parr's Wood High School and Stockport Grammar School. Recorded on Wednesday 11 November (the day after the performance of the opera), the conversation transcribed here deals with both the ideas behind a specific production and the practical problems involved in the work's staging and will, hopefully, not only act as a useful handbook but also encourage others to tackle a work that has, at the time of writing, received only three performances in the UK.

To the obvious delight of those involved, Henze spent many hours during his time at the RNCM listening to rehearsals, coaching and talking to the students performing his music in the concurrent Henze Festival, and running a workshop for young composers from the RNCM and the University of Manchester. The unique photographs by Tony Ward which form an essential part of this book are a record of these rehearsal and workshop sessions.

Those of us who were privileged to meet, and spend time with Hans Werner Henze during his stay in Manchester will not forget the experience of being in the presence of such a remarkable individual. As Henze, in his autobiography *Bohemian Fifths*, remembers his meeting in 1954 with Stravinsky, so we will remember Henze: "the simplicity and directness with which he expressed himself, and that is so characteristic of all great men and women, could not fail to make its effect".

STAGING 'POLLICINO': A CONDUCTOR'S AND DIRECTOR'S PERSPECTIVE

*The following conversation with the conductor Gary Walker [GW]
and the director Jennifer Hamilton [JH] was recorded on the day
following the performance of the RNCM's production of 'Pollicino'.
The interviewer was Douglas Jarman [DJ].*

DJ   Gary Walker, can you tell me about the practical problems you encountered in preparing this production?

GW   The main problems at the beginning were organisational – first of all, we had to persuade people to be involved in the project. I don't believe that the piece can be done by *any* group of children, and one has to draw on resources outside those that a school can normally provide. In the original Montepulciano production, professionals were brought in to help, and the school there was lucky enough to have an inspiring teacher. I was very keen to have motivated children in the production who had, perhaps, had some previous dramatic and musical experience, however small.

There is also the problem of where to find the adult sing-

9

ers. One really needs to have links with a conservatoire or an opera company, or perhaps a strong group of amateur singers.

DJ   And the instrumentalists? Some of the parts are very difficult.

GW   It might be possible to find some of the instrumentalists you need in a fee-paying school, but probably not in a state school, especially now that free instrumental tuition has disappeared. The age of the children also makes a difference. Primary school children are unlikely to be string players of the calibre that the work demands, particularly where string tuition has been cut. Another problem is that percussion instruments, which used to be the backbone of all school music classes, are now less common than electronic keyboards and synthesizers – and there's no place for keyboards and synthesizers in *Pollicino*.

Some of the instrumental parts in the piece are intended to be played by professionals, or at least by adults. Henze suggests that the solo violin part, for example, should be played by an adult and the piano part certainly needs one. In our production, we used a senior pupil from Chetham's [specialist music] School, Manchester to play the concertante violin part, and a student from the RNCM to play the piano.

I was surprised to find that, in the past, children played the percussion parts. Originally, every single instrument had its own part, so there would be twenty or so percussionists all playing separate instruments. Because we already had a lot of children from a number of different schools, we decided that this wouldn't be feasible – we didn't want to create an organisational monster! Besides, with twenty separate players, some would have to wait an inordinate amount of time for their entries. The steel drum, for instance, has to wait half an hour or more before playing, so it's not just a matter of playing the right notes – it's playing them in the right place. You're unlikely to find a conductor who can cue *all* twenty percussion parts separately in addition to all the other orchestral cues – you would need a separate conductor just for the percussion!

To overcome these problems, we condensed the percussion parts so that they could all be played by six students. This obviously makes the individual parts more difficult because, clearly, everyone has more to play – but it was worth all the effort, and it worked.

As far as the orchestral parts were concerned, I have to say that they weren't always clear about instrumental cues. An instruction such as *Tacet Scene 9*, for example, needs additional clarification from the conductor as to where Scene 9 actually starts and ends, as this isn't marked in all the parts. So the conductor has quite a bit of work to do marking up the individual parts from the full score.

DJ   Was the percussion played by schoolchildren in last night's performance?

GW   No, it was played by our [RNCM] students, but having compressed the parts, we didn't have to omit anything apart from about four bars of the triangle part. We found, therefore, that it was perfectly possible to do the whole thing with six percussionists, including a timpanist.

Despite the fact that the RNCM has some superb xylophones and marimbas, we decided to hire Orff-Schülwerk tuned percussion instruments (which Schott generously supplied free) in order to achieve the particular sound that Henze wanted. We should remember that this piece was written for children and that the composer expected neither a 'glitzy' sound, nor a flawless performance. Ironically, staging *Pollicino* in a conservatoire as the gala opening of a highly-publicised festival meant that we were taking a work intended for schools into an environment in which wrong notes and rough edges are not expected, but the fact that our performance lived up to the high standards demanded by the RNCM was the very reason that it was such a success.

DJ   How many were in the orchestra last night, and how many of them were schoolchildren?

GW   Altogether there were about thirty-five, and apart from the six percussion players, the organist, the pianist, the two guitarists and the mouth-organ player, they were all school-children.

Hans Werner Henze and Gary Walker in conversation

DJ   Did you experience any particular problems in getting the orchestra together? The score calls for a number of unusual instruments.

GW   Getting hold of the psalteries was a nightmare! As you are no doubt aware, the psaltery is a pretty rare instrument. I telephoned various contacts and finally tracked down a psaltery teacher here in Manchester – Roger Child – to whom I sent the parts. The first set-back came when he informed me that the parts were unplayable because they were chromatic, and he was only familiar with diatonic instruments. Had Henze made a mistake, or was there a different sort of psaltery in existence of which Roger Child had no knowledge?

We finally got in touch with Henze himself. Although I had met him only once (and then very briefly) at Montepulciano, so hardly knew him, he could not have been more helpful. He replied almost immediately to say that, far from a traditional psaltery, what we needed was a rare form of the instrument made by a firm in Germany. He had chanced across one of them in a music shop and was immediately attracted by its wonderful 'wiry' sound. We contacted the firm through Studio 4 distribution, via Schott, and eventually managed to get hold of three instruments.

Henze's use of the psaltery in the piece is a stroke of genius – one of the things that strikes me most about his music, especially the Sixth and Eighth Symphonies, is his ear for orchestral colour and orchestration. I asked him if he had had a particularly inspiring orchestration tutor, and he replied "No, not at all – bombs and guns!"

The tuning of the psaltery is difficult. I had to tune all three instruments myself before last night's performance. The instrument is simply a set of metal strings which are tuned with a tuning key – it's the same principle as a piano. The long strings are easy to adjust, but with the short strings, the merest fraction of a revolution of the tuning key shoots the pitch up, not a semitone, but a whole octave. Once tuned, however, the psaltery is very simple to play – Henze sent us a very amusing fax (addressed 'From the desk of the Boss') saying that the instrument was so easy that "even I or Professor Gregson could play it" – and that, for me, was the great joy of discovering the instrument.

The crumhorns also presented us with problems, partly because they are rare instruments and partly because it is difficult to find people to play them, especially in schools. As the crumhorns are very prominent in the work – they accompany almost every appearance of the Ogre and often play on their own – they cannot be omitted. In the end, we found oboists

13

and bassoonists to play them, but it required quite a lot of skill and courage for the instrumentalists to make the transfer.

There were one or two further problems. The recorder parts, for instance, had occasionally to be rearranged (or played on different instruments), because some of the notes were off the top and bottom of their range, and at one point, we had to put the xylophone part up an octave. We also found that the guitars were supposed to be playing at the top and bottom of their range at the same time, so their parts needed some adjustment too.

DJ   How long did you rehearse the music?

GW   We were rather late in getting started because of the school summer holidays, and then we had to schedule rehearsals around two weeks' half-term holiday which came immediately before the Henze Festival. Our first full orchestral rehearsal was for four hours and, because there was so much to sort out, we only just managed to get through the whole piece once. We then had a further three four-hour rehearsals, all in the week before the Festival, followed by all-day rehearsals on the Saturday, Sunday, Monday and Tuesday, leading up to the performance on Tuesday night. In addition to the full rehearsals, we had two one-and-a-half-hour rehearsals for recorders and strings only at Chetham's; fortunately, the piece lends itself to being broken down into its constituent parts for sectional rehearsals.

So, to answer your question, we took about six weeks to put the performance together, whereas somebody I know who performed *Pollicino* in Switzerland had four months of rehearsals!

We were very lucky with Tom [Gibson], our Pollicino. Some of Pollicino's arias are very complicated, for example the beautiful 'Listen, our parents have left us'. There's nothing to help the singer here, except possibly the percussion cues – if the singer can hear them. But as the percussion notes coincide

14

with the voice rather than come *before* the vocal notes, they're not really of much help. We simply went over Pollicino's arias so often that in the end Tom was able to pull a note out of the air – we'd say "Sing a D", and he would.

DJ   Did he have perfect pitch?

GW   No, but he developed a sense of timbre, a sense of sound in his head and I'm sure that, as a result of being involved in *Pollicino*, he now has a much better sense of pitch than he had before.

DJ   How did the other children manage?

GW   The brothers also have difficult parts, and while their sense of pitch didn't develop to the same extent as Pollicino's, there is no doubt that it improved – they were, for instance, able to cope with one particular section which is not only complex harmonically but *a cappella* to boot.

JH   We made the point that the children should always sing assertively so that, if anything went wrong, we could try to sort it out. It was important that they didn't feel intimidated by the music – if they did, they tended to sing tentatively and then nothing improved.

GW   At first the children didn't sing because they didn't know the notes and – quite understandably – they only wanted to sing if they could get the music right. We really had to persuade them to sing out loud in order to get started.
    When I first looked at the score I was concerned at how much there seemed to be for the brothers to sing – it's one thing to find one outstanding performer, like Tom, but quite another to find six! However, I soon realised that, once you discount all the acting and the surrounding music, there are probably only about ten minutes when the brothers are actu-

ally singing on their own. You don't notice it in performance – that's one of the things that's so clever about the work – but it's the saving grace as far as the children are concerned.

What I love about this piece is that there aren't any compromises. There are some aspects that are slightly simpler than they might otherwise have been (there aren't, for instance, any 7/8 or 5/16 bars), but there aren't any compromises for anybody – neither for the singers nor the orchestra. Given that it is hard to communicate directly without making concessions, what impresses me about *Pollicino* is that Henze remains both realistic and true to himself.

DJ   We've talked about the singers and their initial reticence, but what about the instrumentalists?

JH   Interestingly, the instrumentalists – the guitarists, for example, whose training is geared towards solo repertoire – had difficulties with things that an orchestral player would find straightforward. At first their playing was too 'internalised', and they had to learn to play in a much more extrovert way. Curiously, it took them time to adjust to the simpler passages that a folk guitarist would have played quite instinctively, while the complex things took less time.

DJ   Where did the instrumentalists come from?

JH   The bulk of the orchestra and the solo violins were from Chetham's School. The psaltery players were from the Royal Northern College of Music Junior School and the pianist, percussionists and the guitarists were all students at the RNCM. So whereas all the young singers came from main-stream schools with good music departments, the instrumentalists all came from specialist music institutions.

DJ   Jennifer, tell me how you set about the production.

16

JH   When Gary and I first went to talk to the schools about *Pollicino* I was very conscious that I was talking to children who were 11, 12, 13 years old and, because my own son is that age, I know that it's an age when it's very important to be 'cool'. I was there to sell to them the idea of their taking part in a fairy story, and I wasn't at all sure how comfortable they'd feel. So I went out of my way to stress the social relevance of the story – I talked about the poverty, about the Father being out of work, about the dysfunctional family, all of them part of society today. I wanted them to see that they were doing something that could be about here and about now.

In retrospect, I probably needn't have bothered. Fairy tales bewitch people. They have a quality which engages the imagination and breaks down prejudices – they tap into something in the subconscious. As soon as we started rehearsals, the children threw themselves into the whole fantasy. One of my specific concerns was whether they might have a problem with dressing up as animals and certainly with the idea of *talking* to animals – after all, they had just moved from primary to secondary school and, naturally, wanted to be perceived as being grown-up. I needn't have worried at all; they loved the whole thing, especially when they got into costume.

DJ   Talking about the animals, what about the Wolf? Does he have to be an adult?

JH   In his essay on *Pollicino*, Henze talks about there being only four adult voices (the Mother, Father, the Ogre and the Ogre's Wife), but the score makes it clear that, of all the animals, the Wolf has to be an adult. Not only does he carry Pollicino on his back, but he has to be larger, more frightening, than the other animals – almost like the Ogre. The Wolf's part is no longer or more complicated than those of the other animals – certainly no more complicated than the Owl's – but it is written for tenor or high baritone voice. In this production, it was played by a student from the RNCM.

DJ Now that we've started talking about the adult roles, can you tell me how you conceived them?

JH Well, perhaps I can best answer that by starting with what I hoped to achieve at the end of the opera. I had an idea that I wanted all the adult characters to come to some sort of a 'resolution' – that the audience should know what they were going to do with the rest of their lives.

You may remember that at one point in Scene 2, the Ogre considers retiring to Hawaii. At the end of our production, with this in mind, I invented the bit of business where the Ogre puts on his Hawaiian shirt, tries a sip of Pina Colada (from a pineapple!), dons his sun hat and sets off for his new life.

Again at the end of the opera, the Ogre's Wife is supposed to faint with shock over the loss of her daughters. However, we have just seen her standing up to her husband for the first time in her life, and I wanted to show her being empowered by this achievement. Indeed, Gabriella [Lambert-Olsson], who played the part, was very much of the opinion that her rage at the loss of her daughters was the trigger for her ceasing to behave like a victim. So in our production, she wakes up from her coma, attacks her husband and chases him out of the house. She is now free to make her own choices and, having lived all her married life on a carnivorous diet, she drools over a vegetarian cookbook while ecstatically devouring an Iceberg lettuce. The point I wanted to make was that obsessions rarely leave us – they just change their guise.

As far as the Mother is concerned, I wanted her to appear at the end of the opera on the far side of the river, watching her children dancing onwards to their new life – and letting them go.

DJ So that the crossing of the river becomes a symbol of their growing up?

JH   Exactly. Henze said that Bruno Bettelheim was one of the sources of inspiration for *Pollicino* and one of the points that Bettelheim makes in *The Uses of Enchantment* is that fairy tales about bad, cruel parents show children that their parents aren't gods, the fairy tales therefore acting as vehicles to help them to achieve separation and, ultimately, to leave home. In rehearsal, we tried having the Mother on the far side of the river to illustrate this idea, but it didn't work and we had to abandon it. Another time perhaps…

DJ   You haven't mentioned the Father yet. I thought that the most upsetting character in the whole opera was not the Ogre but the Father. Do you agree?

JH   Absolutely. I simply couldn't think what to do with him. I wasn't able to imagine him ever developing or 'growing' – he was so resolutely angry and depressed. Even the Ogre has a certain charm. There is a hint of redemption in his character so that, even at his worst, he still has the ability to contemplate being a different person. But the poor Father is unable to imagine the possibility that his life could be any different and, even when his fortunes do change for the better, he sacrifices his children again. Cruelty seems to be his only path. He can't see a way of getting out of the tunnel he's trapped in. His anger is born of deprivation. He treats his wife and children the way he feels the world has treated him. He's the most negative and tragic character in the opera.

DJ   There was a production by English National Opera of Humperdinck's *Hansel and Gretel* at the London Coliseum that was very sinister and emphasised the dark side of the piece.

JH   Yes, and recently I saw a production of the same opera where the mother and the witch were played by the same person. This is quite a popular device. It made me speculate whether the Father and the Ogre in *Pollicino* could be played

19

by the same person, and similarly whether the Mother could also play the Ogre's Wife. It would be perfectly possible with the right singers, and would, I think, be an interesting experiment.

We talked about 'fairy-tale enchantment' earlier, but I also wanted to create a realistic 'family' atmosphere in this production, so that the audience would be aware of the tensions between the Mother and the Father – that their relationship has been damaged by the Father's despair. The Mother is, I think, slightly frightened of her husband and constantly tries to humour him – not unlike the Ogre's Wife. The entire cast took this idea to heart, and the result, I think, was that one really felt for the plight of the children.

The hopelessness of the children's situation is something that's very strong in the music; some of the music in the forest scene, for example, is profoundly bleak. One has to approach this piece with a degree of truth so that one can acknowledge these feelings of despair. The dark, lonely resonances need to be heard and embraced. There is no such thing as 'just a fairy-tale'.

DJ   I agree – it's not simple and straightforward, but a very dark work.

JH   It is a disturbing piece, but not in the way that *Hansel and Gretel* disturbs. I think one feels uneasy in *Hansel and Gretel* because it is so 'sugary'.

DJ   While Humperdinck's music tends to soften the underlying menace, Henze's writing in *Pollicino* doesn't. Henze knows that he's touching on something deep in the subconscious.

JH   I agree. Ultimately I feel more comfortable with this piece than I do with the Humperdinck. We constantly read in the papers about the horrific things that are done to children,

20

and I always feel that Humperdinck doesn't really deal with what is inherent in the subject of his opera. The terror beyond the horrific things in it is made too acceptable.

Henze, on the other hand, takes what underlies the tale of *Pollicino* – the terror, the violence – very seriously indeed. It's true that some of the Ogre's 'nasty habits' are humorously presented to us, but some aren't. The black humour changes into something more nauseous, and therefore more honest. It's interesting that the Ogre is nearly always accompanied by a crumhorn, so that even his most lyrical passages have a queasy, unsettling undertone.

DJ   Of course, since Humperdinck's time, we've not only had Bettelheim but Freud. We've had all the publicity about cases of child abuse. We're far more aware *now* of these dark psychological and social undercurrents.

JH   That's something that we tried to touch on in this production – I don't know if we were successful. Interestingly, it's precisely when the Ogre decides to fatten up the children in anticipation of his feast that he starts to contemplate change. It's significant, I think, that we see that side of him when he's at his most rapacious. I talked to Toby [Stafford-Allen] who played the Ogre about this. It is as if the Ogre is as much driven by obsession as the Father. He has appetites and desires which can never be satisfied; he is as discontented as the Father.

We created a moment in the production where the Ogre instinctively makes a move to pat a child's head, and is completely unable to do it because the sense of the child's vulnerability and innocence disturbs him too much. I was thinking of Claggart in *Billy Budd*, someone else who finds vulnerability and innocence so profoundly disturbing that he's not equipped to deal with it and, as a result, becomes monstrous.

The Ogre's Wife is equally interesting because she's so hysterical.

Jennifer Hamilton and Hans Werner Henze in conversation

DJ   Is that stipulated in the score?

JH   Not in so many words, but I think the music makes her mental state quite clear. When she sings alone, in recitative, the music is almost like plainsong, but when she's with the Ogre she appears to me to go crazy. I tried to make her not so much a caricature as a real woman who has become psychotic through living with this dreadful husband. Of course Gabriella is Swedish – from the land of Ingmar Bergman – so she loved all this! She was immediately in tune with the idea of playing the piece as a fairy story, but at the same time making its darker meaning clear.

DJ   And the children responded to these darker undercurrents?

JH   Yes, they did, and in a completely natural way. When they're first abandoned in the forest, frightened and alone, with the music creating a strong sense of unease and bewilderment, the children immediately start to sing a folk song and, suddenly, to play games. They don't analyse the change of mood, they just *do* it – it's a very cleverly-handled moment in the opera – and this is typical of the way children respond to that kind of traumatic situation. It's partly displacement activity, and partly an indication of their tremendous instinct for survival, both physical and emotional, which I found very moving.

DJ   Was there any aspect of the opera that the children found particularly difficult?

JH   Interestingly, the only area where they seemed to feel genuine awkwardness was over the love interest between Clotilde and Pollicino. I think that perhaps they are reaching an age when it is all a little too close to home. In the duet where Clotilde and Pollicino first meet each other, and Pollicino says to Clotilde 'You're nice,' and she replies 'Do you think so?', both young people were so squeamish and embarrassed that I said 'OK, if that's how you feel, why don't we show it? Say the words and look away as if you're embarrassed.' So Tom would say his line and then rush away down stage as if his life depended on it. By getting the children to play out the gaucheness they obviously felt, this whole scene became very charming.

The end, however, was more difficult; it was too intimate for them to cope with. We therefore decided to move the action on fairly quickly in order to avoid becoming sentimental. It wasn't worth making the children feel exposed – they were obviously uncomfortable with the romantic ending, and forcing the issue would have spoiled all the spontaneity of the excellent work they'd done.

DJ   Did working with children create other problems that you would not normally have encountered?

JH   I found it very stressful because everyone, including the orchestra, was being challenged to the hilt. It's a challenge that can drive a director to extremes of rage and stress because one's dealing with so many different things.

For example, when the orchestra became bewildered and weren't clear what they were doing, they would lose focus and would immediately start looking out of the window, or in mirrors, and so on – that was their way of responding to difficulties.

When the children 'lost it', they would become manic and career around all over the place, with the result that one had to spend a lot of time and energy rounding them up and settling them down again. Once or twice I shocked myself when trying to accomplish this – I sounded like the Ogre's Wife! But they seemed to forgive me.

They were consistently good-humoured – and so creative. They came up with so many excellent ideas, one of which was in the game of hide-and-seek when one of the boys can only find a couple of sticks to hide behind, and does so in the earnest hope that nobody can possibly see him. That was Giles's idea, and it brought the house down – a real *coup de théâtre*.

Had we had a longer rehearsal period, I would have liked to use even more of their ideas, some of which were rather complex and many of which were extremely difficult technically. Unfortunately, we simply did not have the time to explore them all. Sometimes I had to say 'Let's leave that and think about it later', because the psaltery players, for instance, had to leave the rehearsal at seven o'clock – and I hated doing that.

One of the main practical problems was drawing up a rehearsal schedule and sticking to it. We arranged sectional rehearsals so that we didn't have everyone sitting there from five o'clock onwards, but almost immediately the schedule would disintegrate – because a child was late, or somebody's car wouldn't start. There was always a good reason, but even so, it put enormous additional pressure on us because it left us with people sitting around with nothing to do. Actually, I seemed to care about it more than the youngsters did – they did their homework, gossiped, ate crisps. They never complained.

DJ   Were all the rehearsals outside school hours or were you able to use some school time?

JH   They were all outside school time.

DJ   So the children would have done a day's work at school – and you'd have done a day's teaching – and then you would all turn up for rehearsal?

JH   Yes. I think that the members of the orchestra found that particularly difficult – after all, the singers were at least doing something different from what they'd been doing during the day. The children in the orchestra had already spent a day sitting in class, and then they had to sit through rehearsal all evening. We asked so much of them in terms of concentration.

DJ   How did the children learn their parts – did you teach the singers their parts with the piano first?

JH   A team did that, and towards the end of the rehearsal period, I started involving them in the interpretation.

DJ   How many rehearsals did you have in all?

JH   Well, in addition to the ones that Gary mentioned, I had three or four sessions with the adult soloists and Pollicino during the half-term holidays. This arrangement worked very well, and I recommend it to anyone doing the piece. If you can rehearse with the core singers – Clotilde, Pollicino, the Wolf, the Owl and the adults – they learn the 'geography' both of the piece and the production, and are able to act as ringleaders and teachers, so that it is much easier to 'filter in' the other singers. Their parts are complicated enough, and if one asks them to come into rehearsals without the help and support of the key singers, it all becomes very difficult.

DJ   Having seen this production in the round, I can't imagine the work being done on a proscenium arch stage. In the Concert Hall here at the RNCM, you were able to have the musicians on stage. You could use all the space around and through the audience; one could see the children working their way back through the audience picking up the pebbles as they found their way home. Your production turns this piece into real music theatre – it asks people to accept it on its own terms, not as a play with music.

JH   In a production in the round, not everyone sees everything, but that doesn't matter because everyone has a different, individual view of the action. What was so special about our production was that the children gave a 'real' performance – they *lived* it – so when they moved through the audience and one could observe them close at hand, one could not fail to be impressed by their total involvement in the piece.

At the performance, I found myself sitting next to one of the places Pollicino dropped one of his pebbles, and just the picking up of that pebble was an entire mini-performance in itself. It was like having the special option of a close-up shot on the TV. I was delighted to see that Henze also happened to be sitting where a pebble had been dropped and so he also had a similar, 'private' performance – I could see that he really appreciated that moment. Those people sitting at the top of the auditorium would have missed those particular details, but then they would have experienced different things, such as the children on their path to the woods. And of course, their perspective on the whole performance would have been quite different from that of the audience lower down, as I realised myself when I went up to check the Stage Right sightlines during the final rehearsal.

Staging *Pollicino* in a concert hall, as we did, creates its own problems. The RNCM Concert Hall does not have theatre lighting, for example, so a lighting rig had to be brought in and installed and consequently we lost a whole day's rehearsal. Furthermore, there are no wing spaces as in a theatre, so the children needed chaperones to escort them all round the building. I have always loved the venue as a space, but it's not without problems in terms of co-ordinating and cueing. Our production looked like a workshop performance but it was more labour intensive, and much harder work.

DJ I can see that there must have been the further problem of performers having to make their entry through the auditorium doors. Outside the concert hall, there are people walking around, talking, having coffee and so on – the singers are in the middle of that at one moment, and the next moment they are suddenly on stage. Did they find it difficult to make such a sudden, difficult mental switch?

JH I was very worried that the children would be distracted, and not recognise what are quite complex musical cues – like their first entrance which is cued in by the first violin. The instrument is soaring up into the ledger lines, and it's easy to think it has reached the peak of the phrase before it has. But in fact the children got it right every time except once, and that was at a rehearsal when their chaperone panicked and sent them on too early. The extent to which the children could focus their attention astonished me.

DJ   It sounds as though you had a good time, despite all the hard work, and that you found the whole enterprise very rewarding.

JH   Oh, I did – and it was! Despite wishing I didn't care so much about other people's opinions of my work, I think I generally tend to look for approval – I like people to *like* what I do. With this production of *Pollicino*, however, I can honestly say that the real 'praise' and reward for me was the children's response to what they were doing; they were glowing with their achievement, and it was entirely infectious.

Irrespective of what anybody might say or think about the production, I got such enormous satisfaction from helping to create an experience as a result of which so many children – and adults – felt good about themselves, and proud of what they'd made. Everybody should experience that at least once in childhood... and preferably more than once.

HRH The Duchess of Kent confers Fellowship of the RNCM on Hans Werner Henze

HANS WERNER HENZE, FELLOW OF THE RNCM: A PRESENTATION ORATION

Anthony Gilbert presents the composer to the President of the RNCM, HRH The Duchess of Kent, for conferment of a Fellowship on 12 November 1998.

Madam President...

It is my honour to present the distinguished composer Hans Werner Henze, an introduction of pure formality since to any-one interested in contemporary opera, music theatre or ballet, in the survival of the symphony or the concerto in the twenti-eth century, in contemporary vocal writing, in contemporary chamber music or, in fact, in any classical genre, Henze will need no introduction at all. The output is tremendous, and spans over fifty years – indeed Henze was internationally known when I was a raw student, and hungry absorption of his scores at that time contributed significantly to my own development as a composer.

In his early years he was associated with the so-called 'Darmstadt' school of *avant-gardists* but, finding his own personal voice, soon became impatient with their doctrinaire views and in 1953 left Germany altogether for Italy, where he has lived and worked ever since.

Not that he has ever compromised: recognition and success came to him early, but they came on his terms. As we have been hearing this week, the music speaks with a power and authority, a humanity and passion that transcends idiom. He has the poet's capacity to be on the one hand intensely autobiographical, without yielding to self-indulgence, or on the other, politically trenchant, and his 'Italianate' lyricism is matched by a Germanic attention to detail and formal logic.

Henze's connections with this country are long-standing. He attracted the attention of our critics in 1958 with his beautiful work *Kammermusik*, in which he directed Peter Pears, Julian Bream and the Melos Ensemble at Aldeburgh, and with his ballet *Undine*, choreographed by Frederick Ashton for Covent Garden that same year, Margot Fonteyn dancing in the title role. I can remember the raves; they began a love-affair with British audiences which resulted in performances here of three major operas in short order: *Elegy for Young Lovers*, *The Bassarids* and the extraordinary 'action for music', *We Come to the River*.

Given his early break-away from the mainstream of European *avant-garde*, it is perhaps unfair to draw comparisons with his Darmstadt contemporaries; but one factor does link him with several of them: his passionate support, through his music, of radical left-wing causes. *We Come to the River* is a prime example of such a work, but there are others, notably the virtuoso baritone work *El Cimarrón*, and the oratorio *The Raft of the Medusa*. At early performances of this work, a riot-police presence was required because of its inflammatory effect on the audience. His consciousness of music as an instrument of subversion probably developed during his youthful years under the Nazi régime. And if, in his later works, political steel has been tempered by satire, everywhere the composer's intense personal feelings are evident – perhaps no more so than

30

in his *Requiem* which was written in memory of his long-standing friend and champion, Michael Vyner.

For a normal composer, the writing of nine symphonies, sixteen operas, nineteen works for solo instrument and orchestra, eleven ballet scores and a considerable range of vocal, chamber and instrumental pieces would take far more than the fifty-plus years of Henze's working life so far. But Henze is not a normal composer, so we must not be surprised to find him also directing international festivals – notably the Cantiere at Montepulciano, the youth festival in Styria, and the Munich International Festival of New Music Theatre, all of which he founded. Or teaching at centres of international distinction such as Cologne and Tanglewood. Or doing a considerable amount of conducting – he is, for instance, permanent guest conductor of the Berlin Philharmonic, and directs performances of his own work all over the world.

All this has been recognised by distinguished awards too numerous to list in full. His first honorary Doctorate was awarded by the University of Edinburgh as early as 1971; his most recent by the University of Osnabrück in 1996. He is an honorary member of the Accademia Santa Cecilia in Rome, of the Salzburg Academy of Sciences and Arts, of the International Society for Contemporary Music, and of the American Academy and Institute of Arts and Letters. He has been awarded the München Leuchtel Gold Medal, and further special cultural awards from the same city of Munich; the Sibelius Gold Medal; the Grand Cross for Distinguished Service of the Order of Merit of the German Federal Republic...

Madam President, we could spend the second half of the concert like this – but now, it is my great honour to present **Hans Werner Henze** for admission to Fellowship of the Royal Northern College of Music, *honoris causa*.

Gary Walker conducts while Jennifer Hamilton watches the
Dress Rehearsal of 'Pollicino'

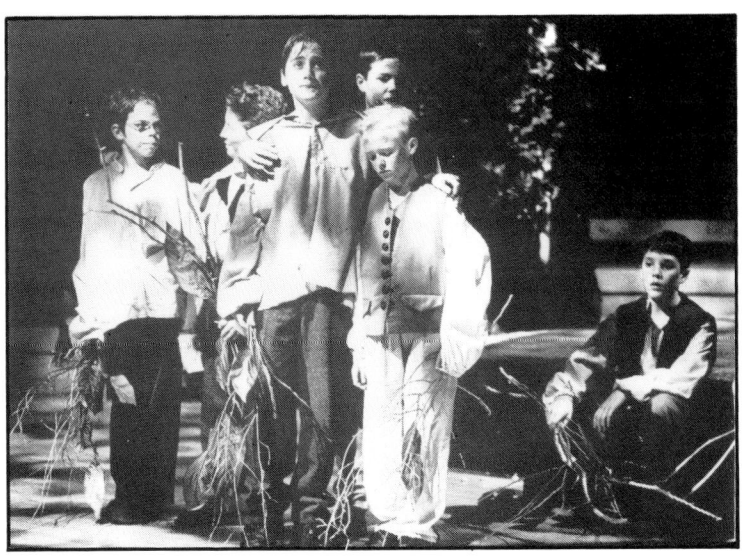

Pollicino and his brothers abandoned in the wood;
Dress Rehearsal of 'Pollicino'

Hans Werner Henze talks to Tom Gibson [Pollicino] after the performance

The cast of 'Pollicino' with the composer

The Mother serves supper to Pollicino and his brothers in Scene 1

35

The composer signs programmes for the cast after the performance of 'Pollicino'

CONVERSATIONS WITH HENZE: I

Hans Werner Henze [HWH] *in conversation with Douglas Jarman* [DJ] *at the RNCM on 13 November 1998*

DJ   Maestro Henze, can we start by talking about the development of your musical language? You grew up at a time when it was difficult to hear new music. What did you hear as a young man and how did your language develop from that?

HWH   Do you mean at the beginning?

DJ   Yes.

HWH   Well, it has been extraordinary to hear so many of my works played over the past few days – recent pieces, and also very early ones like the *Kammersonata* that we heard at lunch-time, or the *Concertino* for piano and wind that we heard last night. The *Concertino* dates from 1946/7 – immediately after the war – when, in spite of the end of the régime, a young composer in Germany had great difficulty in getting to know new music, contemporary music, because it wasn't available in music shops or in the libraries. It simply wasn't there. So we had to wait for it to come from abroad.

I was in the lucky situation that, not far from Heidelberg, where I was studying between 1946-48, was Baden Baden, the 'capital' of the French-occupied zone of Germany, where the radio station was controlled by the French Army. The man who ran it was a Captain Ponnelle, Pierre Ponnelle (father of Jean-Pierre, the stage designer). Whenever he came back from Paris, Pierre Ponnelle brought new scores for the radio orchestra. In this way, I heard my first Messiaen and other French composers of the time, and also Stravinsky's latest neoclassical works. Then the first Schoenberg arrived. I remember my confusion when I heard the Septet – the one with three clarinets, I believe – and how very difficult it was to understand and to like. At the same time, I was carried away with the beauty of Alban Berg's Violin Concerto, which was a great discovery.

I particularly remember hearing Stravinsky's *Orpheus* for the first time. It was the first German performance of this piece, and I attended the rehearsals and saw the extraordinary score – very sparse, with just a minimum of information in it. Very impressive. The serious, deep neoclassicism of Stravinsky's score of *Orpheus* had in it, in my opinion, a kind of suggestion for young composers about how they could come to grips with the knowledge of music of earlier times, and how to communicate using – in the case of *Orpheus*, for example – the forms of the early baroque and Renaissance.

There were enormous contradictions and contrasts in the music of the first part of our century, contradictions and contrasts that we eventually learnt about, and learnt from; all this, of course, is part of the formation of one's own language. Sometimes, one can only absorb these pieces by writing something that stems directly from the original model, like young painters who copy paintings in museums – that sort of approach is, I believe, a fair comparison. I used to think that one could detect the provenance of my earlier works quite easily but now, with the distance of time, I don't believe that it is all *that* easy, because there are so many different influences in them.

This morning, for instance, I heard a rehearsal with the BBC Philharmonic of my First Piano Concerto which I hadn't heard since 1952 [laughter] – for the simple reason that it was never played again [laughter] – so the Manchester Festival kindly agreed to put it on! In this work I can hear, quite clearly, the influence of Schoenberg's Piano Concerto and the kind of techniques he uses – his thirds and octaves, and so on. I don't know whether other people will hear it in the same way; we shall have to see.

The First Piano Concerto is only two years older than the *Concertino* that we heard the other day, so you can see how quickly things develop and change. One tries to absorb experiences and include them in what one day might become a personal style. On the other hand, when I listen – as I have been doing all this week – to the new and the old together, I sometimes have the feeling that I haven't really learnt very much in the last fifty years [laughter]. Something, however, always remains the same – perhaps that is what they call 'style' [laughter]. I don't know... maybe.

DJ   Can I just take you up on that last remark? I was going to come to 'style' later, but now that you have mentioned it, I'd like to ask you what 'style' is. There's a passage in Berlioz's *Memoirs* where the composer describes the characteristics of his style. I happened to notice a newspaper report this week that called you a 'chameleon' and I want to ask you what you feel are the characteristics of Henze's music that make it Henze's?

HWH   Oh, that is not for me to say... [laughter]

DJ   Ah well, perhaps I'd better move on! Can I, then, ask you about your relation to the German tradition? It seems to me that you, more than any other living composer, embody

the German tradition. You have carried on writing symphonies; you write in traditional genres – there are the string quar-
tets, we heard the Piano Trio yesterday, and so on – and you
continue to be interested in traditional forms, especially sonata form. What is it about sonata form that still fascinates
you and holds your interest?

HWH Well, that's not difficult to say. I think that with
Beethoven, whose constructive thinking goes further than his
predecessor Haydn's, there comes this extraordinary idea of
developing musical phenomena from a small, central kernel,
with the music always emerging and growing from a principal
thought – it's almost like somebody thinking out loud, thinking through a form, a theory.

And there is the idea of a contrasting element – like an
important idea in a play, something dramatic, something human, something not abstract that appears as an opposed or
'different' element. And the involvement of the two materials
is the most important musical, artistic event in the sonata.

There is this wonderful story – I don't know whether it's
true or not but it is very nice and also rather impressive – that
Alban Berg, as a teacher, criticised a pupil for bringing in the
reprise as a literal repeat of the exposition, just as it was at the
beginning of the movement. Berg said to his pupil: 'That is
impossible – you can't do that. Don't forget, these themes and
these ideas have been through so much drama, so much trou-
ble, that they *can't* be the same. They have been changed by
what they have gone through.'

So, you see, there is this idea of changing, and developing.
It's a very dynamic principle. People used to say that it's a
characteristic of the German school – Brahms, the same with
Schoenberg. Schoenberg even created a 'method' from this idea
– whether for the better or the worse as regards the creative
inventiveness of composers is another story [laughter]! But
the idea of constant change – of ideas, of form, of the rotation
of musical thought and phenomena – *that's* what I find the

most important and most interesting aspect for myself. I'm not saying that it is the most fantastic discovery, or something that younger colleagues should regard as a 'recipe' for how to compose. Not at all. The only thing I would recommend to younger composers is that they *think* about the fantastic possibility of developing ideas; writing not suites, but drama [pause]. I'm talking too much – I'm sorry!

DJ   No, not at all! That's why you are here! I was going to ask you about the musical forms in your operas because, seen in this light, sonata form (with its need for recapitulation) and opera aren't incompatible. The drama has moved on, but the music has also changed its meaning. All your operas have quite strict formal structures behind them, but I suppose *The Bassarids* is the most obvious example.

HWH   Yes, *The Bassarids* is a symphony.

DJ   Yes. How did that come about? The libretto from Auden and Kallman arrived out of the blue. You didn't have any say in it.

HWH   No, but, of course, I had told them that I wanted them to write me a four-movement symphony.

DJ   Right, so it wasn't just a happy coincidence?

HWH   No. There was the responsibility of reading these highly poetic and visionary verses and feeling, eventually, obliged to try to live up to them. But what happens ideally and philosophically in *The Bassarids* is, I think, absolutely wonderful. Wonderful.

DJ   I'm particularly interested in this because it's a very Bergian way of handling opera. Berg is the only other composer that I can think of who imposes these strict forms on his

41

dramatic structures.

The other link with the German tradition that I wanted to ask you about concerns both Berg and, perhaps more importantly, Mahler. There seems to be a strong link between that Mahlerian/Bergian tradition and your own music in a number of ways. Firstly, there's a transcendentalism in your music (as in the Sanctus at the end of the *Requiem* that we heard the other night) that seems to come from Mahler, or perhaps Bruckner. But there is also – and I mean this as a compliment – a kind of 'impurity'; yours is a music that is willing to take in everything, to create a kind of synthesis – a music that tries to embrace the world. That seems to me to be a very Mahlerian idea. Do you agree?

HWH Yes. I'm very glad you have mentioned this – it's very kind of you [laughter]! When I was getting to know the music of the first part of our century, one heard Mahler's name but not, of course, his music, which was not allowed to be played or performed at that time. I heard my first Mahler *years* after the Second World War, and I remember it very well. It was on my car radio – wonderful music – and I stopped and turned off the engine and waited. It was raining outside, and inside there was this *wonderful* piece and I didn't know who the composer might be – Janácek, Elgar – I had no idea at all. So I waited for the end of the piece and I learnt that it was Gustav Mahler's Ninth Symphony. You couldn't get *anything* of Mahler's on record in those days. So gradually, by listening to radio broadcasts or even driving to places where there were Mahler symphonies on the programme, I would absorb these works.

It's very difficult to describe what an impression this music made on me. Even now, in my writing (not only my symphonic writing but even in *Pollicino*) there is *always* some Mahler. Gustav Mahler, for me, was like a hero who tells you that you have permission to compose freely. Don't believe what the snobs say, and don't believe what the doctrinaire schools say: just go ahead and do it, and the more frankly you express yourself, and the more openly you express yourself, the nearer you will come to the truth of artistic behaviour and artistic creativeness.

DJ   We're going to hear your Sixth Symphony tonight and I wanted to ask you to talk a little about that piece. It comes from that period in the late '60s and early '70s when you were writing your most overtly political works and when there was a kind of political excitement that, I think, students nowadays would find quite difficult to imagine – a period when we really *did* feel that we could change things. What is interesting about the piece, and about all those overtly political pieces, is that there are no concessions in your musical language. [HWH: No!] I find that interesting because there were some composers in England during that same period who, for example, started writing little pieces in C major based on *The East is Red*. But you have never compromised. I wanted to ask you about that whole idea of politically committed music, what it means? Can music be politically committed *without* a text?

HWH   Good question! I think the human intention behind the musical composition influences the sort of effect that it makes. The symphony that can be heard tonight – *beautifully* played, between you and me [laughter] – is in a new version which was first performed some years ago by Ingo Metzmacher with the Munich Philharmonic. It used to be in one movement but I've now made three movements out of it, so there are two intervals for the listener to gather breath, so to speak.

It was a piece that I was commissioned to write for the Cuban National Orchestra and it was premièred there in, I think, 1969. I conducted it. We had almost a month of rehearsals. It was very hard for the musicians there – judged by international standards, they weren't the very best – and it took a great deal of time to rehearse to a point at which, somehow, it worked. Some composer colleagues at the radio station

43

put a lot of reverberation on the broadcast and managed to 'improve' the sound of the orchestra [laughter]. I have this tape... [more laughter]. You know, I *could* have chosen New York or London or Berlin, or some such place, for the première of my Sixth Symphony but I wanted *that* particular place.

I also wanted to learn as much as possible from this revolution, which was such a moving thing, especially for European intellectuals. It looked as though there would be a new way, a way of creating socialism properly. There was a lot of personal freedom and there was the idea that every citizen is an individual who has the right to develop his talent freely, supported by the nation. It looked, in those years, as though there was a wonderful new possibility of paradise on earth. I'd go as far as to say that.

Hans Werner Henze makes a point to Douglas Jarman

I was in Cuba twice. The first time, the idea was to write a piece for the National Orchestra and do some teaching and some composing. I did all that and so I knew the audience. I heard a concert given by the National Orchestra. They played Shostakovich, which is slightly easier (not *very* easy, but easier), and so I knew the kind of audience that I would have: a lot of young people – in fact the majority of the audience – who had a natural curiosity about everything to do with the arts. In Cuba, as opposed to the Eastern Bloc countries (Russia or East Germany), modern music in the sense of *real* western modern music, was not forbidden, was not taboo. Quite the opposite. One tried to learn from that, and to advance the ideas of revolutionary music with the technical means of advanced western music.

New York was the point of reference for the Cubans – Cage, Earle Brown, those sorts of people. That was their orientation. A lot of the music that my Cuban colleagues wrote had revolutionary lyrics, but there was also a lot that was purely music as such. For instance, there was a composer called Juan Blanco who wrote electronic music. He was always asked to provide music – electronic music – for mass rallies, or when they opened a new hall, or when a newly-built village was inaugurated. So he would create fantastic electronic music, with loudspeakers on all the surrounding hills, and so on. Very modern – but they would all think 'Esa es la música (revolucionaria)'– it *was*: electronic music for the crowd, not for the midnight *élite*, but for the masses.

That was music *without* words. The sound in itself becomes a language, the expression of something, the replacement of something. So I wrote this symphony in the way I did in order to understand my own feelings about what was happening at that time, and I thought that I was really reflecting the energy and the 'youngness' of this country – the cheerfulness, the exuberance of the people, who are not only hard-working, but also *happy*. I didn't want to do what Mendelssohn did with the *Italian* or the *Scottish* symphonies. I felt I had to *go* there and describe *my* personal dilemma – my moral and social dilemma – in *my* terms, otherwise it would have been a completely senseless enterprise.

So my style, my language in these pieces is an attempt – I don't know whether it comes across or not – to change, to improve: to become less of a decadent westerner, and more powerful, more energetic – *younger*. I wanted to be *younger*! That didn't work at all [laughter]! But when I hear the music of the Sixth Symphony, as I did yesterday in rehearsal, I have the feeling that, within the context of my own technical limitations at that time, I took an important step forward in my musical creativity.

I'm talking all the time, Douglas!

DJ   Yes, you're supposed to be [laughter]! I can remember that, at the time, improvisation itself was seen as a kind of political act; it was a way of allowing the performers to be empowered. A lot of your pieces of that period – *El Cimarrón, Natascha Ungeheuer* – have improvisation or graphic notation in them. Are you tempted to re-compose, or to write those sections out in the way that you have done in the Sixth Symphony?

HWH   Yes. I mean, improvisation then was very *chic* – it was also very timesaving [laughter]! If you use improvisation as I did in *El Cimarrón*, you have wonderful drama and the performer has two-and-a-half minutes to show how fantastic he is. OK. But on the whole, instrumentalists do *not* like to be invited to improvise. They don't like it *at all*. They think: 'We'll play what you write, but we won't compose for you. That's not our job' [laughter].

I remember, there was an old *mulatto*, a little man, who played the piccolo trumpet with the National Orchestra in Havana. At my first rehearsal, when we got to the point where the improvised section began, I said, 'Now you can play what you like' and the trumpet-player replied 'Well, in that case I shall play *La Cucaracha*!' [a popular Latin-American song – laughter].

In the new version of my Sixth Symphony that you will hear tonight – if you don't go home before [laughter] – I have eliminated some improvisations that I, at least, found slightly embarrassing. I think that they were embarrassing to the players too because, as I've said, they don't like to improvise. So now I've composed them. I've turned them into written music, to my greatest delight [laughter]. It makes the piece much more *interesting*, all the way through.

DJ   I'd like to ask you about opera and politics. You've managed to write operas that have a strong political content – I'm thinking of the Edward Bond works in particular, because Bond is a tough political writer – and you have written them for the mainstream opera houses. Now Brecht thought that you couldn't do that; he thought that, if you wrote for the opera house, the Establishment would control and defuse what you produced. But you've done it. We've even had *We Come to the River* at Covent Garden!

HWH   Yes, I know. But they didn't know what it was going to be like when they accepted [laughter]! But, of course, *We Come to the River* did have some more productions after that, on the continent, and even one in America. And in 2000 it will be done at the Salzburg Festival. I think that as these things age, they acquire a distance; they seem to be of less immediate relevance, and can therefore be done in comfortable social surroundings.

DJ   There is one question I particularly wanted to ask you. Over thirty years ago, in *Music and Politics*, you said: 'I cannot tell, at any rate not yet, how I visualize the role of music in our time'. I wondered if, almost forty years later, you could now visualize its role ?

HWH   I can, a little bit. Would you like to hear what I think?

DJ   I would love to hear it [laughter]!

HWH   Well, I think I have learnt one thing, perhaps because I've done a lot of educational work with children and with young composers during the last twenty or more years. The one thing I have learnt for myself, to a point where I can even talk about it and recommend it to young composers, is to consider music as the only language of the mind and of the soul that we have as human beings. It is the *only* approach that we have to the subconscious. So it is an important part of being human – not a 'medicine' exactly but *very* helpful – and the more human beings *know* music, and *about* music (perhaps even *create* or *compose* music themselves), and the nearer we get to this amazingly clear and not very mysterious world of sounds and metaphors, the closer we approach this extraordinary but 'unspeakable' language of music.

I think that one of the most important concerns of a modern society should be to help people in schools, for instance, to learn as much music and as much *about* music as soon as possible. They should be encouraged to do this *not* by listening but by actually *performing* music, by coping with notes, by writing them, by trying to sing and play them. We should communicate with one another by making music ourselves.

So, if I were a child, I would understand how great pieces such as Mahler's Third Symphony are, because I would realise how little *I* was able to do. I would understand the proportions of profundity and *grandeur* much better if I were able to follow a piece with a score, for instance, or were to have the chance of trying to write music like Mahler's, at least for a while. That would make me want to strive for knowledge of this extraordinary thing which is music, and of how it works in the context of the human mind.

At least since Freud's time, and the appearance of psychology and psychoanalysis, we have known that there are important links between the profundity of the soul – of every human soul – and the mysterious effect that good music has when it reaches deeply into the mind of the listener.

DJ   I was going to ask you a further question, but that was such a wonderful answer that I think that we should end to-

48

night's conversation there. I would, however, like to say one further thing before we finish. There is a point in your autobiography where you talk about sitting next to Stravinsky at a performance, and being aware that you were in the presence of history. I think that all of us here tonight, and indeed all of us at the Royal Northern College during this Henze Festival, have felt that we are similarly in the presence of history. We are very privileged, and very grateful to you. Thank you very much, Maestro.

The composer with Clark Rundell and members of the RNCM's New Ensemble at a rehearsal of Henze's 'Requiem'

Henze conducts the RNCM Brass Ensemble during a rehearsal of his Sonata for Eight Brass, watched by James Gourlay

Henze at a rehearsal of his Piano Quintet

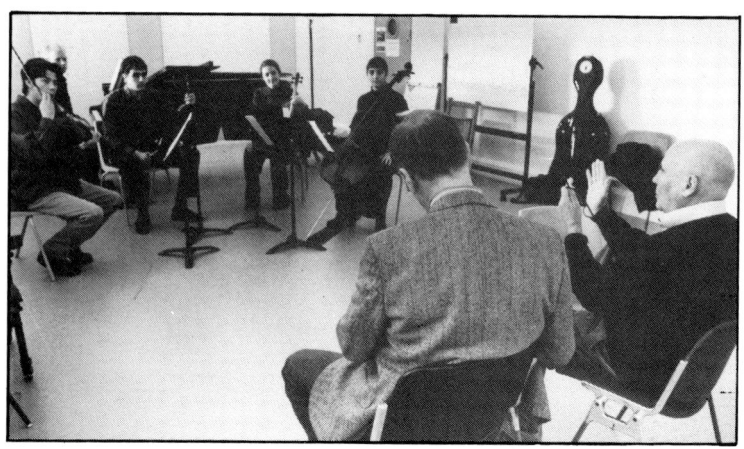

*Henze and Christopher Rowland with the Gurney Quartet and
Jeremy Young (piano) during a rehearsal of Henze's Piano Quintet*

Student Alda Lee plays Henze's 'Cherubino' (3 miniatures for piano) to the composer and Renna Kellaway

Henze discusses his 'Fünf Nachtstücke' with pianist Caroline Jaya-Ratnam and violinist Alex Afia

Students Alex Afia and Caroline Jaya-Ratnam rehearse Henze's 'Fünf Nachtstücke' watched by the composer

CONVERSATIONS WITH HENZE: II

Hans Werner Henze [HWH] *in conversation with Peter Sheppard Skaerved* [PSS] *at the RNCM on 14 November 1998*

PSS   Through the whole of my performance life I have been involved with the music of Hans Werner Henze; I think that the first of his pieces that I performed was *Il Vitalino radoppiato*, a piece in which the musical conversation degenerates into argument. You talked a little last night, Maestro, about the formal musical structures in your operas but there often seems to be some kind of hidden drama operating in your chamber music, where there is no written text. How far should the performer get involved in the underlying meaning, especially when he has to grope to find it?

HWH   If we're talking about chamber music we are dealing with the most intimate things. We're talking of monologues, 'soliloquies' – I can't say it properly, but you know what I mean! The composer consciously writes monologues for instruments. If you are writing for a large orchestra, the technical demands are of a different sort from when you're writing for only one or two players. But even with an orchestra, I want the performers to know what I *meant* to say, to involve them with the right notes, to involve them as human beings. The larger the orchestra, the less solo communication is demanded. It's a very different process from chamber music, where communication is at its most complicated.

PSS   The Eighth Symphony, which we're going to hear tonight, seems to demand a chamber music aesthetic. There is one point, for example, when a string quartet emerges and then fades back into the orchestral texture.

HWH   In the second movement? Well, the second movement represents the nocturnal goings-on between the divine Titania and Bottom the tailor. Bottom, you remember, has been transformed by Puck into an awful stinking donkey and Titania has fallen in love with him. The donkey is represented by the brass – especially the trombones (what else?) – and they produce a really 'horny' sound [laughter]! For Titania, I use the strings to say the things she says in Shakespeare. You can follow the dialogue between the strings and the awful brass noises. The strings express an exaggeratedly sweet emotion, which builds up in pitch until it reaches tackiness – and then suddenly, there are these solo strings.

This is the best way to remind the audience that there are very intimate feelings involved, that it is *real* love that Titania feels for this beast, that these are genuine emotions. I wanted to direct the intellectual sense towards intimacy. But only for as short a time as was necessary. So the string quartet idea emerges – and disappears again, as soon as the message is delivered.

PSS   There's a big difference between that and the Solo Violin Sonata, where the soloist has to represent a whole cast of characters.

HWH   Yes, the Sonata is a real piece of theatre. It's a scene from the first Italian secular play, the *Fabula di Orfeo* by Angelo Ambrogini, the Tuscan poet called Il Poliziano (he was born in Montepulciano!). If you remember, there are the three clowns, three rustics, Mopso, Tirsi and Aristeo, the last of whom brings death by mistake to Eurydice. They have been strolling about the countryside when they suddenly come across Eurydice the nymph – walking in a field of grain, a vineyard, or perhaps an olive grove – and go after her. Mopso and Tirsi continue to clown around; they remain light-hearted and funny. But Aristeo is more sinister. He's going to get her, and starts chasing after her. Eurydice realises what's happening and runs away. She's just reached the edge of the wood, to hide, when she treads on a viper. The last note of the Sonata is her scream of death when she steps on the snake.

PSS   Is it necessary for the audience to know this story?

HWH   No, but it's nicer [laughter]!

PSS   So it helps to know the background?

HWH   Well, if I may put it like this: I like Beethoven's Fourth Piano Concerto more and more every time I hear it. That's because I have learnt more about *my* life and more about *Beethoven's* [laughter]!

Let me talk a bit more about my Eighth Symphony which is, as you know, based on Shakespeare's *A Midsummer Night's Dream*. The first movement is about Puck putting a 'girdle round the earth' in thirty minutes. It's made up of three elements. The first is the baritone line – the equivalent of an operatic aria – which represents Oberon telling Puck to get him the flower from the west. Or rather I *should* say, from the *south*, because I devised a construction plan for this movement that reflects the journey harmonically. That is the second element – the harmonies, which stand for the sand, desert and the sea, and so on. The third element comes from Puck's travelling orders – 'I'll put a girdle round the earth...'. You can *hear* this girdle. It goes from the North Pole [HWH makes a falling, circular gesture of the hands at this point], starting with sharp, crystalline instruments, and then flies down until, four minutes later, it arrives at the South Pole, as denoted by the deepest instruments; then – by way of a shrill trumpet solo – it ascends back to the North Pole again. All the while, there is continuous semiquaver and demisemiquaver movement, even in the lowest instruments, to depict the 'girdle'. At the very end, the music comes back in retrograde, and *there* is Puck with the flower which he gives to Oberon – you can hear him, you can almost *smell* the flower in the orchestra.

Hans Werner Henze and Peter Sheppard Skaerved

The second movement is a dance in which the mood is always changing. It consists of the dialogue between the Donkey and Titania – I've already talked about that.

The last movement – and here I'm returning to your question, Peter – is a setting of Puck's speech at the very end of the play: 'If we shadows have offended...' and so on. The music here follows Shakespeare's lines and ideas in the form of melodic procedures, and behaves as though Puck and his colleagues are apologising for the short-comings not only of the characters in the play, but for those of my symphony and the audience – and it offers forgiveness and love – for the audience, for myself, and for *anyone* else who cares to have it [laughter]!

PSS   It seems to me that you are interested in instrumentalists being on the edge both of their abilities and the possibilities of their instruments for much of the time. Is that true?

HWH   Well, why shouldn't instrumentalists get exhausted too – the composer did [laughter]! The 'almost impossible' is *always* interesting in music. It's a bit like a circus act – will she, or will she not, fall from the rope? Will Peter Sheppard get the harmonic at the very end of the third movement right? Usually, you know, that last note is played too short [more laughter]!

PSS   You're talking about that last note of the Violin Concerto, aren't you? It's *very* exposed, almost unplayable – it's a *horrid* note!

HWH   Maybe it's a misprint [laughter]! But, you see, I care for the well-being of my players!

PSS   You've sometimes said that in order to depict beauty, you must also depict ugliness in order to arrive at an appreciation of beauty.

HWH   Of course, one way to depict beauty is the boring way [laughter]! It's to do with music being a language. One way of being beautiful is being ugly. We realise now how deeply music relates to the psyche. Ever since the discovery of psychoanalysis, we have realised *how* important music is, even for a non-musician.

But I want to say something more about instrumentalists, especially since we have instrumentalists here. My first musical studies were in Brunswick, in a small conservatoire – timpani was my subsidiary instrument, my major was piano (which I've never mastered properly) – and I lived in a room with six other people of the same age. One was studying the bassoon, another was a trombonist, another was learning the violin, and so on. Their main concerns were understanding *what* the musical text was about and *how* to play it correctly. So, I've come to respect instrumentalists since childhood.

Instrumentalists are the most important people in music-making, and without them, we are all *nothing*; we can forget the whole thing. I have always admired instrumentalists, and appreciated how they have to work throughout their lives to maintain and sharpen their skills.

Instrumentalists want to understand what they are playing. And if you tell them what, and why, they are playing – once they understand – then the sound changes; it becomes much closer to what the composer had imagined and had heard in the inner ear when he composed the piece in question.

The composer has to do *everything* possible to make scores clear and inviting for the players in order to keep their interest. If instrumentalists complain that they have nothing to do, then one is simply not writing good music. Look, in the theatre, the characters on stage understand the story; they can see what the other actors are doing, and how they fit into the play. It's the same with an orchestra. If everyone in the orchestra knows what the trombones are doing in the second movement of the Eighth Symphony, they *immediately* become mentally more involved.

PSS We are talking about beautiful scores which inspire the player. What is your original starting point?

HWH When I start, I have a blank sheet in front of me, but I *know*, from the start, which instrument is going to play, so I have the sound in my ear from the outset – say, the sound of a single violin in my head, which I sketch onto the paper. Then over the next few days, I will develop it and so on – I will have to make a proper violin part. But I think of my players; I care for my players and I want to give them the possibility of producing of their best. They *want* to be involved and so I try to involve them. When I write something I think, for example, of the second oboe player in the Berlin Philharmonic – he hardly ever has a solo and so I write him a little something, I put some nice solo notes into his part, to cheer him up.

Musicians, instrumentalists, are intellectuals of a particular kind. They are not only dealing with the complex structures of the music of our time, but they also have an understanding of history, of style. And it's an understanding that is not static but constantly developing. They balance the joy of playing, moving and developing with the constant process of thinking about music. It's wonderful if musicians know why they are doing what they are doing – it's an involvement that they want and deserve. Without instrumentalists there is nothing. The performers are our closest allies.

Peter, I have been talking a lot – what is the time? I think it's time for me to stop.

PSS   Yes, I'm afraid it is. It has been an enormous pleasure to talk with you. I'm sure that we shall all remember these conversations and learn from your experiences. Maestro, thank you for being with us tonight, and thank you for composing music that both challenges us and gives us such pleasure.

Hans Werner Henze, November 1998

Second-year composition student at the RNCM, Paul Clay, discusses his saxophone quartet 'Craze' with Hans Werner Henze after its performance by Havoc at a Composers' Seminar/Workshop

The composer relaxes with RNCM students after a performance

The composer studies the score of his Piano Quintet

Elgar Haworth conducts the RNCM Symphony Orchestra at the rehearsal of Henze's Sixth Symphony (revised version)

A trio of composers with their editor at the Henze Festival. From left to right: Anthony Gilbert, Hans Werner Henze, Sally Groves (Head of Contemporary Music at Schott & Co., London) and John Casken

Henze at the RNCM, with Fausto Moroni Henze

Hans Werner Henze with Professor Edward Gregson, Principal of the Royal Northern College of Music

TO THE RNCM FROM HWH...

Hans Werner Henze

Professor Edward Gregson
Royal Northern College of Music
124 Oxford Road
Manchester M13 9RD

c/o Renate Doufexis
Roseggerstraße 15
60320 Frankfurt/Main
Tel. 0 69/5 60 24 50
Fax 0 69/56 59 42

17.11.1998

Fax-No. oo 44 161 273 76 11

Dear Eddie,

last week in Manchester, I have had the good
fortune to learn what a Royal College can be like.
An astonishing number of excellent performances was
to be heard, excellent in a way that one can en-
counter only very rarely in the outer world.

I was deeply moved, and still am. May I ask you to
let the students know that I feel much admiration
for their technical skills and that I'm most grateful for their dedication and for their obvious
(and very audible) engagement in playing these
difficult scores and bring their meaning across
to the listeners.

Thank you, dear students of the RNCM,
and good luck to you all!

Yours ever,